W9-BXY-249

Seaside Circles

written by **Molly Dingles**
illustrated by **Neale Brodie**

dingles & company New Jersey

For Mike McCann

First printing

PUBLISHED BY dingles&company

P.O. Box 508 • Sea Girt, New Jersey • 08750
WEBSITE: www.dingles.com • E-MAIL: info@dingles.com

LIBRARY OF CONGRESS CATALOG CARD NO.: 2004095732
ISBN: 1-59646-033-4

Printed in the United States of America

ART DIRECTION & ORIGINAL SERIES DESIGN BY Barbie Lambert
ART DIRECTION AND DESIGN BY Rizco Design
EDITED BY Andrea Curley
EDUCATIONAL CONSULTANT Maura Ruane McKenna
ART ASSISTANT Erin Collity
PRE-PRESS BY Pixel Graphics

Molly Dingles is the author of *Jinka Jinka Jelly Bean* and *Little Lee Lee's Birthday Bang*, as well as the Community of Color and the Community of Counting series. She is a writer and lyricist who holds a bachelor's degree in fine arts/theater from Mount Saint Mary's College and a master's degree in educational theater from New York University. She lives in Manasquan, New Jersey, with her husband, David.

Neale Brodie is a freelance illustrator who lives in Brighton, England, with his wife and young daughter. He is a self-taught artist, having received no formal education in illustration. As well as illustrating a number of children's books, he has worked as an animator in the computer games industry.

The Community of Shapes series is more than just a series of books about shape identification. The series demonstrates how individual people, places, and things combine to form a community. It allows children to view the world in segments and then experience the wonderment and value of the community as a whole.

What is a Circle?

Technical definition:
A closed flat figure bounded by a curved line that is equally distant from the center.

Kid-friendly definition:
A flat shape that is perfectly round.

Circular
wagon wheels

Circle-shaped sandwich bun

Circular beach ball floating

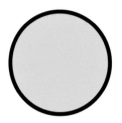

Circle-shaped shining sun.

Circle-shaped
sand dollar

Circular oranges
for a snack

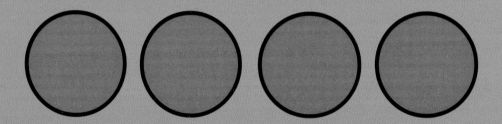

Circles on a bathing suit

Circular volleyball
to smack.

Circle-shaped beach badges

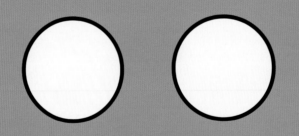

Circular pebbles in the sand

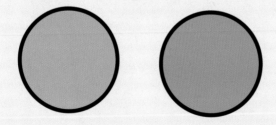

Circle-shaped scoops of ice cream

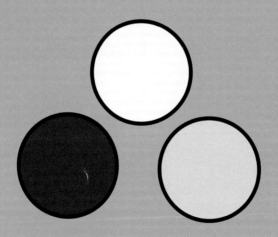

Circular jellyfish in hand.

Circular shapes are all around.

circle beach   circle beach

ABOUT SHAPES

Use the Community of Shapes series to teach your child to identify the most basic shapes and to help him or her relate these shapes to objects in the real world. ASK:

- What shape is this book about?
- How many circles are there in the beach scene?
- Identify the biggest circle in the beach scene. Now the smallest.
- What is your favorite circle-shaped item? Why?

ABOUT COMMUNITY

Use the Community of Shapes series to teach your child how he or she is an important part of the community. EXPLAIN TO YOUR CHILD WHAT A COMMUNITY IS.

- A community is a place where people live, work, and play together.
- Your family is a community.
- Your school is a community.
- Your neighborhood is a community.
- The world is one big community.

Everyone plays an important part in making a community work – moms, dads, boys, girls, police officers, firefighters, teachers, mail carriers, garbage collectors, store clerks, and even animals are all important parts of a community. USE THESE QUESTIONS TO FURTHER THE CONVERSATION:

- Have you ever been to a beach, lake, or pool? If so, did you have fun?
- How are the people in the book different from one another? How are they the same?
- How is the community in the book similar to your community? How is it different?
- Describe your community.

OBSERVATIONS

The Community of Shapes series can be used to sharpen your child's awareness of the shapes of objects in their surroundings. Encourage your child to look around and tell you what he or she sees. ASK:

- Can you find circle shapes in your house?
- Can you find circle shapes outside of your house?
- What circle-shaped object do you use most often?
- What kind of everyday objects (found inside or outside) could you use to make circles?

TRY SOMETHING NEW ... Help stop water pollution. See if you and your parent can pick up trash at a beach, lake, pond, or stream in your neighborhood. Make sure you wear gloves.